EMPOWERMENT JOURNAL

AFFIRMATIONS AND
DECLARATIONS FOR
AUDACIOUS
LIVING

JANIA AMARA

SUITTE

A Goshen Publishers Book

Empowerment Journal:

Affirmations and Declarations for Audacious Living

ISBN: 978-1-7342639-4-7

Copyright ©2020 Jania Amara Suitte
Library of Congress Cataloging-in-Publication Data

All rights reserved solely by the author. The author guarantees all content is original and does not infringe upon the legal rights of any other person or work. No part of this book may be reproduced, shared in a retrieval system, or transmitted in any form or by any means, electronic, mechanical, photocopying, or recording, without prior written permission of the Author or Publisher.

Published in 2020 by:
GOSHEN PUBLISHERS LLC
P.O. Box 1562
Stephens City, Virginia, USA
www.GoshenPublishers.com

Our books may be purchased in bulk for promotional, educational, or business use. For inquiries please contact the publisher via email: Agents@GoshenPublishers.com.

Photos by Angela Hardy

"Positive J.E.M.S." logo by Christopher Thomas

Cover designed by Goshen Publishers LLC

Printed in the United States of America

All Scriptures are quoted from the King James translation of the Bible unless otherwise noted. All term definitions are retrieved from dictionary.com unless otherwise noted.

EMPOWERMENT JOURNAL

AFFIRMATIONS AND DECLARATIONS FOR AUDACIOUS LIVING

JANIA AMARA

SUITTE

DEDICATION

This book is dedicated to my Lord and Savior, Jesus Christ, for loving and redeeming me, and for endowing me with special gifts. He is trusting me to make a difference. It is for everyone who is ready to walk in boldness, reach their goals, and walk in their destiny. It is especially for those who might lack the confidence to do so.

ACKNOWLEDGEMENTS

I am most grateful that the Lord blessed me with my parents, James and Janice, who give me unwavering support and guidance daily. With their love and encouragement, I am confident that I have all I need to make the world a better place.

Many other people support me in my effort to empower others to audacious living:

- My Grandparents: James and Nay Ruth Suitte
- My Auntie: Renee' Keyes
- My Cousins: Chris and Andre Smith
- My Godparents: Sharon Greene and David Ralph, Esq.
- Family and Friends

AUTHOR'S NOTE

There are things in life that will stand in the way of our happiness and joy. Do you know that true happiness and joy are already in us for us to embrace?

When we believe in ourselves, reject the lies spoken against us, and recognize when people are not supportive of our gifts, then we can enter that place of our purpose here on earth.

We have to stand up and speak up for what we want and for what is right. We have to speak positively about ourselves and other people.

Showing kindness toward each other is essential in order to build each other up. That takes courage, acts of faith, and a willing heart. That's what bold and audacious living is all about! Are you up for the challenge?

It is not always easy because it involves our emotions. The University of Rochester Medical Center states that **journaling** helps deal with overwhelming emotions because it's a healthy way to express yourself. Using the model in URMC's Health Encyclopedia, I designed this *Empowerment Journal* to help you do that.

- **Try to write every day.** Set aside a few minutes every day to write. This will help you to write in your journal regularly.

- **Make it easy.** Keep a pen and your *Empowerment Journal* handy at all times. Then when you want to write down your thoughts, you can.

- **Write your responses to my affirmations and declarations.** Your journal doesn't need to follow any certain structure. Let the words flow freely. Don't worry about spelling mistakes or what other people might think.

- **Use your journal as you see fit.** You don't have to share your journal with anyone. If you do want to share some of your thoughts with trusted friends and loved ones, you could show them parts of your journal.

I would love to know how this *Empowerment Journal* helps you. Please leave me comments at

https://www.goshenpublishers.com/jania-suitte

(1)
Find your joy and peace in the midst of the storm. They will provide comfort.

(2)
Joy awaits you. Jump for it!

(3)
I declare that I will be a bountiful blessing to everyone in my circle.

(4)
I declare that the seeds that I sow in others
will increase in abundance
and big blessings will come to me.

(5)
I am a dream builder, a vision embracer,
a motivator for success,
and I will walk in it to the fullest.

(6)
I shine and radiate when I walk into a room.
I am that force that will
shed light on any situation.

(7)
Be courageous.
Be strong.
Be a shining star!

(8)
Tap into your inner most beauty and smile. You were created for marvelous works.

(9)
Continue your faith walk even when the load is heavy. You will break down barriers and see the fruits of your labor.

(10)
When you are feeling broken and in despair, remember WHO is the glue that is holding you together.

(11)
I will get my power walk on and be fierce about it.

(12)
Visualize all that you can accomplish
and then seize the moment.
It is yours to reach!

(13)
Intelligent, remarkable, and astounding should be my birth names.

(14)
I am blazing with boldness and I am a creative cultivator. I will seize the opportunity to use my gifts to build people up.

(15)
Embracing the little things in life
will set you up for the big blessings.
Greater is coming.

(16)
Success in life is not determined by the riches you have, but rather by the love you share with others.

(17)
Display a loving, kind heart on a consistent basis and watch it become contagious.

(18)
Sometimes making decisions can be tough.
Stick with those decisions
so that people will take you seriously.

(19)
You matter!
You have a voice!

(20)
Popularity is temporary.
Being who you are and what God called you
to do will be eternal.

(21)
That beautiful person you see in the mirror is strong, brave, and courageous.

(22)
Walk with your head up.
There is no time for a pity party.

(23)
I am breaking down barriers, casting away fears, and walking into my purpose.

(24)
Be unforgettable by being a seed planter and not a seed stomper of dreams.

(25)
Encourage someone
and watch your own blessings blossom.

(26)
Celebrate the best you inside and out.
You were born to lead.

(27)
You were created to do great things.
Your execution will be timely.

(28)
In your weariness,
dig deep to find inner strength.
It will propel you to soar.

(29)
I am a creative innovator
that is destined for greatness.

(30)
Fears be gone!
I remove them right now and replace them with fearless faith.

(31)
Negative words won't hurt me.
They bounce off like a ball hitting a wall.

(32)
There is no lack in my life,
just love that pours out daily in abundance.

(33)
A good friend will encourage you, stand up for you, laugh with you, and cry with you.

(34)
Upgrade your contacts periodically and surround yourself with positive mission-minded people who are going places.

(35)
Keeping my head up as I embrace what life has for me will allow me to see various paths for success.

(36)
There is an enormous amount of joy in my heart and I will preserve it to fight against hatred.

(37)
I must expand my reach
and grab hold of the enormous blessings
that God has for me.

(38)
When life isn't fair and disappointment comes, turn the situation around by rejoicing, dancing, and singing.

(39)
Dance, even if you don't consider yourself a dancer. Movement is powerful for the mind, body, and soul.

(40)
Take a leap of faith
and make your dream a reality.
What are you waiting for?

(41)
Speak it.
Believe it.
Achieve it.

(42)
When the Lord's light shines on your face, your heart will suddenly start to race.

(43)
When you dream of things in life to do,
remember that God chose you.
Pave the way for others.

(44)
Reach higher so you can grow mightier.

(45)
Be bold.
Be audacious.
Be YOU!

ABOUT THE AUTHOR

Jania Amara is very talented and creative. She enjoys writing, arts & crafts, dancing, singing, gymnastics, and cheerleading. Her mission is to help people step out of their shell and pursue their goals in life. She wants people to be touched and blessed by the Lord with guidance on their journey.

Jania Amara believes that everyone has their own story to tell and they should follow their own golden path in order to be successful in life. She also believes that people should be comfortable with themselves and not try to be like anyone else. People should not tear each other down with negative words, be jealous, or bully others.

While a middle school student, she launched into entrepreneurship with her first business, *Positive J.E.M.S.* Her business name stands for Jesus Empowers My Soul and it is based on the scripture, "For we are God's handiwork, created in Christ Jesus to do good works, which God prepared in advance for us to do" (Ephesians 2:10).

The Lord blessed Jania Amara with her business to:

- Empower young girls and women to use the gifts that God gave them;
- Spread motivation and positivity; and
- Build self-esteem and confidence.

Jania Amara resides in Northern Virginia with her parents (James and Janice) and two dogs (Baxter and Gigi).

To contact or follow Jania Amara, listen to her podcast, order her book, or audio chat with her, visit her webpage:

https://www.goshenpublishers.com/jania-suitte

Made in the USA
Middletown, DE
11 January 2021